TRAVERSE
THEATRE

SCOTLAND'S NEW WRITING THEATRE

Traverse Theatre Company
in association with the Tron Theatre Glasgow

Melody

by Douglas Maxwell

Cast in order of appearance

John	Bryan Lowe
Melody	Lynn Ferguson
Olive	Una McLean
Ashley	Mhairi Steenbock

Director	Lorne Campbell
Designer	Jon Bausor
Lighting Designer	Philip Gladwell
Composer	Max Richter
Voice Coach	Ros Steen
Stage Manager	Lee Davis
Deputy Stage Manager	Gemma Smith
Assistant Stage Manager	Sarah Holland
Wardrobe Supervisor	Maggie Scobbie

First performed at the Traverse Theatre
Friday 10 March 2006

A Traverse Theatre Commission

TRAVERSE THEATRE

Artistic Director Philip Howard

The Traverse is Scotland's new writing theatre. Founded in 1963 by a group of maverick artists and enthusiasts, it began as an imaginative attempt to capture the spirit of adventure and experimentation of the Edinburgh Festival all year round. Throughout the decades, the Traverse has evolved and grown in artistic output and ambition. It has refined its mission by strengthening its commitment to producing new plays by Scottish and international playwrights and actively nurturing them throughout their careers. Traverse productions have been seen worldwide and tour regularly throughout the UK and overseas.

The Traverse has produced over 600 new plays in its lifetime and, through a spirit of innovation and risk-taking, has launched the careers of many of the country's best known writers. From, among others, Stanley Eveling in the 1960s, John Byrne in the 1970s, Liz Lochhead in the 1980s, to David Greig and David Harrower in the 1990s, the Traverse is unique in Scotland in its dedication to new writing. It fulfils the crucial role of providing the infrastructure, professional support and expertise to ensure the development of a dynamic theatre culture for Scotland.

The Traverse's activities encompass every aspect of playwriting and production, providing and facilitating play reading panels, script development workshops, rehearsed readings, public playwriting workshops, writers' groups, discussions and special events. The Traverse's work with young people is of supreme importance and takes the form of encouraging playwriting through its flagship education project *Class Act*, as well as the Traverse Young Writers' Group. In 2004 and 2005, the Traverse took the Class Act project to Russia and also staged *Articulate*, a pilot project with West Dunbartonshire Council for 11 to 14 year olds.

Edinburgh's Traverse Theatre is a mini-festival in itself
THE TIMES

From its conception in the 1960s, the Traverse has remained a pivotal venue during the Edinburgh Festival. It receives enormous critical and audience acclaim for its programming, as well as regularly winning awards. In 2002 the Traverse produced award-winning shows, *Outlying Islands* by David Greig and *Iron* by Rona Munro and in 2003, *The People Next Door* by Henry Adam won Fringe First and Herald Angel awards before transferring to the Theatre Royal Stratford East. Re-cast and with a new director, *The People Next Door* has since toured to Germany, the Balkans and New York. In 2004, the Traverse produced the award-winning *Shimmer* by Linda McLean and a stage adaptation of Raja Shehadeh's diary account of the Israeli occupation of Ramallah, *When the Bulbul Stopped Singing*. This play won the Amnesty International Freedom of Expression Award 2004, appeared in January 2005 as part of the Fadjr International Theatre Festival in Tehran and toured to New York in Spring 2005. The Traverse's Festival 2005 programme received a total of 12 awards, including a Fringe First for its own production, *East Coast Chicken Supper* by Martin J Taylor.

www.traverse.co.uk

COMPANY BIOGRAPHIES

Jon Bausor Designer

Jon trained at Exeter College of Art and Motley Theatre Design Course. For the Traverse: *In the Bag*. Other designs for theatre include *The Soldier's Tale* (The Old Vic); *The Hoxton Story* (Red Room Productions); *Cymbeline* (Open Air Theatre); *The Last Waltz Season* (Oxford Stage Company/Arcola Theatre); *Frankenstein* (Derby Playhouse); *Bread and Butter* (Tricycle Theatre); *Sanctuary, The Tempest* (Royal National Theatre); *Winners/Interior, The Exception and The Rule, The New Tenant, The Soul of Chi'en-Nu Leaves Her Body* (Young Vic); *The Taming of the Shrew* (Theatre Royal Plymouth/Thelma Holt Ltd national tour); *Carver* (Arcola Theatre/RADA); *Tartuffe, Ghosts in the Cottonwoods* (Arcola Theatre); *The America Play* (RADA); *Switchback, Possible Worlds* (Tron Theatre); *The Tempest, What the Women Did* (Southwark Playhouse). Designs for dance include *Before the Tempest…After the Storm, Sophie/Stateless* (Linbury/Royal Opera House); *Mixtures* (English National Ballet/Westminster Abbey); *Non Exeunt* (Ballet Boyz/Sadlers Wells). Designs for opera include *The Queen of Spades* (Edinburgh Festival Theatre); *Cosi Fan Tutte* (Handmade Opera) and *King Arthur* (New Chamber Opera).

Lorne Campbell Director

Lorne trained at the Traverse Theatre on the Channel 4 Theatre Director's Scheme from 2002–2004 and has been Associate Director since 2005. Other training: RSAMD (MDra) and Liverpool John Moores (BAhons). Productions for the Traverse: *In the Bag, The Nest*. Associate Director for *East Coast Chicken Supper* and *The People Next Door* (Balkan Tour 2004) and Assistant Director for *Outlying Islands, Dark Earth, Mr Placebo, Homers* and the *Slab Boys Trilogy*. Other theatre credits include *The Dumb Waiter, Death and the Maiden, An Evening with Damon Runyon, A Comedy of Errors, As You Like It, Journey's End* (Forge Theatre); *The Chairs* (RSAMD); *The Cheviot, The Stag and the Black, Black Oil* (Taigh Chearsabhagh).

Lynn Ferguson *Melody*

Lynn trained at RSAMD. Theatre credits include *The Good Woman of Setzuan* (Royal National Theatre); *A Better Day* (Theatre Royal Stratford East); *Creature from the Mermaid's Purse* (Communicado); *Heart and Sole, Frank, Kindling* (Guilded Balloon); *Mental* (Glynis Henderson Productions). Television credits include *Blessed* (Phil Macintyre Productions); *The Bill* (Talkback Thames); *No Angels* (World Productions). Film credits include *Chicken Run* (Aardman Animation Ltd); *Honest* (Pathé). Radio credits include *Millport, Aria, Kindling, Stanley Baxter and Friends* (Radio 4). Lynn won the Stage Award for Acting Excellence in 1995 and a Fringe First in 2001.

Philip Gladwell Lighting Designer

For the Traverse: *In the Bag*. Other theatre credits include *Macbeth* (Derby Playhouse); *Paper Thin* (Kali Theatre Company); *The Morris* (Liverpool Everyman); *The Canterville Ghost* (Peacock Theatre); *A Whistle in the Dark* (Citizens Theatre); *Bodies* (Live Theatre); *Jack and the Beanstock, Aladdin* (Hackney

Empire); *Hot Boi!* (Citizens Theatre/Soho Theatre); *Tape* (Soho Theatre); *Mother Courage and Her Children* (Nottingham, Bristol, Ipswich); *Bread and Butter* (Oxford Stage Company); *Awakening, Another Fire: America* (Push at Sadler's Wells); *Dreams from a Summerhouse* (Watermill Theatre, Newbury); *The Tempest* (Royal National Theatre tour); *Interior/Winners, The Exception and the Rule, The New Tennant, When the World was Green, A Night at the Circus, Pantheon of the Gods, Young Hamlet, The Soul of Chi'en-Nu Leaves Her Body, Streetcar to Tennessee, Prinaries* (Young Vic); *Way Up Stream* (Derby Playhouse); *Modern Love* (Queen Elizabeth Hall); *Unite for the Future* (Old Vic); and *Dead Funny* (Nottingham Playhouse). Future productions include *Into The Woods* (Derby Playhouse).

Bryan Lowe *John*

Bryan graduated from QMUC in July 2005. Theatre credits include *Kvetch, Honk, Passing Places, Junk, The Winter's Tale* (QMUC); *Beach* (QMUC/Boilerhouse). Television credits include *See No Evil* (Granada); *Waking the Dead, Sea of Souls* (BBC). Radio credits include *Storm Warning* (BBC School Radio); *McLevy* (Radio 4).

Douglas Maxwell Writer

Douglas was Scottish Arts Council Playwriting Fellow at the Traverse from 2003–2004. His previous productions include *Helmet* (Traverse/Paines Plough); *If Destroyed True* (Dundee Rep/Paines Plough); *Mancub* (Vanishing Point); *The Backpacker Blues* (Oran Mor); *Variety* (Edinburgh International Festival/Grid Iron); *Decky Does a Bronco* (Grid Iron); *Our Bad Magnet* (Tron Theatre/Borderline Theatre Company). Douglas was also International Festival Fellow at Edinburgh University from 2002–2003.

Una McLean *Olive*

Una trained at RSAMD. For the Traverse: *Shimmer,* the *Slab Boys Trilogy, Family, The Architect, Sky Woman Falling, Blending In, Ines de Castro*. Other theatre includes *The Kerry Matchmaker, Oklahoma, Annie* (Perth Theatre); *The Vagina Monologues* (Edinburgh Festival Theatre/Theatre Royal Glasgow); *Five Blue Haired Ladies Sitting on a Park Bench* (National tour, Brian Hewitt-Jones); *Beauty Queen of Leenane, Paddy's Market* (Tron Theatre); *Perfect Days* (Borderline Theatre Company); *Albertine in Five Times* (Clyde Unity Theatre); *Lovers, The Steamie* (Royal Lyceum Theatre, Edinburgh); *Mrs Warren and a Passionate Woman* (Pitlochry); *Bourgeois Gentilhomme* (Dundee Rep); *Couples* (Cacciatore Fabbro, Edinburgh Festival); *Revolting Peasants* (7:84); *Beggar's Opera, Fiddler on the Roof* (Scottish Opera). She has played pantomimes for 25 consecutive years including *Cinderella, Snow White, Aladdin* and *Babes in the Wood*. Television work includes her own shows *Did you see Una?* and the children's series *Captain Bonny*. Scottish Television profiled Una in an hour-long *Artery* special, *Numero Una*. Film work includes *Strictly Sinatra* (Universal Focus); *Nan* (Scottish Screen); *The Debt Collector* (Film Four/Pine Film); *Small Moments* (The Short Film Factory). Una was awarded a Doctorate of Letters In 1995 from Edinburgh's Queen Margaret University College and an MBE in 2006.

Max Richter Composer

Max Richter is a graduate of Edinburgh University, The Royal Academy of Music and a student of the late Luciano Berio. For the Traverse: *When the Bulbul Stopped Singing*. Records include five discs for Decca Classical, along with releases on Virgin, BBC Late Junction, Big Chill and FatCat, and collaborations with Future Sound of London, Roni Size and Vashti Bunyan. Films include *Soundproof* (BBC 2006), *Geheime Geschichten* (ZDF 2002), and Ridley Scott's *Future Thoughts* (1998), as well as the forthcoming film from Krzysztof Piesiewicz, writer of Kieslowski's *Three Colours* trilogy. Together with Bach and Arvo Pärt, Max's music made up the score for the recent BBC/HBO landmark production *Auschwitz: Inside The Nazi State*. Further syncs include new films from Robin Williams/Armistead Maupin, and Michael Tully. Currently he is working on *SIBERIA*, a three-hour music and film project for live performance, with Turner Prize Nominee Darren Almond and scoring *Deep Water* for FilmFour/Pathé/APT. Future projects include new music to accompany the films of the late Derek Jarman. Max's solo CDs, *Memoryhouse* and *The Blue Notebooks* (featuring Tilda Swinton) have been widely acclaimed and his third album *Songs from Before* will be released in 2006 with musings by Robert Wyatt and texts by Haruki Murakami.

Ros Steen Voice Coach

Ros trained at RSAMD and has worked extensively in theatre, film and TV. For the Traverse: *I was a Beautiful Day, East Coast Chicken Supper, In the Bag*, the *Slab Boys Trilogy, Dark Earth, Homers, Outlying Islands, The Ballad of Crazy Paola, The Trestle at Pope Lick Creek, Heritage* (2001 and 1998), *Among Unbroken Hearts, Shetland Saga, Solemn Mass for a Full Moon in Summer* (as co-director), *King of the Fields, Highland Shorts, Family, Kill the Old Torture Their Young, Chic Nerds, Greta, Lazybed, Knives in Hens, Passing Places, Bondagers, Road to Nirvana, Sharp Shorts, Marisol, Grace in America*. Other theatre credits include *Mystery of the Rose Bouquet, A Handful of Dust, Cleo, Camping, Emanuelle and Dick, A Whistle in the Dark, A Little Bit of Ruff* (Citizens Theatre); *The Graduate, A Lie of the Mind, Macbeth, Twelfth Night, Dancing at Lughnasa* (Dundee Rep); *The Wonderful World of Dissocia* (Edinburgh International Festival/Drum Theatre Plymouth/Tron Theatre); *Uncle Varick, Playboy of the Western World* (Royal Lyceum Theatre, Edinburgh); *The Small Things* (Paines Plough); *Mancub* (Vanishing Point). Film credits include: *Greyfriars Bobby* (Piccadilly Pictures); *Gregory's Two Girls* (Channel Four Films). Television credits include *Sea of Souls, 2000 Acres of Sky, Monarch of the Glen, Hamish Macbeth* (BBC).

Mhairi Steenbock Ashley

Mhairi trained at RSAMD and Le Coq School, Paris. Theatre credits include *Blues for Mr Charlie* (Tricycle Theatre); *Philoctetes* (National Studio); *On Passe dans Huit Jours* (Paris Teatro); *A Midsummer Night's Dream* (Cottiers); *Marat/Sade* (The Arches). Film credits include *O Jerusalem* (Creative Partners); *Green Street* (Yank Productions); *Ripper 2* (H3O); *Wilbur Wants to Kill Himself* (Sigma/Zentropa); *Young Adam* (Recorded Picture Company). Television credits include *Missing* (Scottish TV); *Murphy's Law* (Tiger Aspect); *The Trouble with Love, Casualty* (BBC).

SPONSORSHIP

Sponsorship income enables the Traverse to commission and produce new plays and to offer audiences a diverse and exciting programme of events throughout the year. To find out more about how to support the Traverse please contact Ruth Allan or Vikki Graves 0131 228 3223/ development@traverse.co.uk.

We would like to thank the following companies for their support:

CORPORATE SPONSORS

With thanks to:

Claire Aitken of Royal Bank of Scotland for mentoring support arranged through the Arts & Business Mentoring Scheme.

Purchase of the Traverse Box Office, computer network and technical and training equipment has been made possible with money from The Scottish Arts Council National Lottery Fund

LOTTERY FUNDED

The Traverse Theatre's work would not be possible without the support of

The Traverse Theatre receives financial assistance from

The Calouste Gulbenkian Foundation, The Peggy Ramsay Foundation, The Binks Trust, The Bulldog Prinsep Theatrical Fund, The Esmée Fairbairn Foundation, The Gordon Fraser Charitable Trust, The Garfield Weston Foundation, The Paul Hamlyn Foundation, The Craignish Trust, Lindsay's Charitable Trust, The Tay Charitable Trust, The Ernest Cook Trust, The Wellcome Trust, The Sir John Fisher Foundation, The Ruben and Elisabeth Rausing Trust, The Equity Trust Fund, The Cross Trust, N Smith Charitable Settlement, Douglas Heath Eves Charitable Trust, The Bill and Margaret Nicol Charitable Trust, The Emile Littler Foundation, Mrs M Guido's Charitable Trust, Gouvernement du Québec, The Canadian High Commission, The British Council, The Daiwa Foundation, The Sasakawa Foundation, The Japan Foundation

Charity No. SC002368

Sets, props and costumes for

Melody

Created by Traverse Workshops
(funded by the National Lottery)

LOTTERY FUNDED

Production photography by Douglas Robertson

Print photography by Euan Myles

For their continued generous support of
Traverse productions, the Traverse thanks:

Habitat; Marks and Spencer, Princes Street; Camerabase;
BHS and Holmes Place.

Traverse Theatre – The Company

Ruth Allan — Development Associate
Aaron Butler — Second Chef
Lorne Campbell — Associate Director
Andy Catlin — Marketing Manager
Laura Collier — Artistic Administrator
David Connell — Finance Manager
Jason Cowing — Bar Café Executive Manager
Jennifer Cummins — Front of House Manager
Maureen Deacon — Finance Assistant
Martin Duffield — Box Office Manager
Suzanne Graham — Literary Development Officer
Hannah Graves — Head Chef
Vikki Graves — Development Officer
Mike Griffiths — Administrative Director
Gavin Harding — Production Manager
Philip Howard — Artistic Director
Natalie Ibu — Marketing & Press Assistant
Aimee Johnstone — Bar Café Duty Manager
Kath Lowe — Deputy Front of House Manager
Norman Macleod — Development Manager
Kevin McCune — Senior Bar Café Duty Manager
Euan McLaren — Deputy Electrician
Katherine Mendelsohn — Literary Manager
Sarah Murray — Administrative Assistant
Dave Overend — Literary Assistant
Emma Pirie — Press & Marketing Officer
Pauleen Rafferty — Finance & Personnel Assistant
Claire Ramsay — Assistant Electrician
Renny Robertson — Chief Electrician
Mairead Smith — Bar Café Duty Manager
Phil Turner — Technical Stage Manager
Alan Wilkins — Young Writers Group Leader

Also working for the Traverse: Alice Boyle, Amy Breckon, Doug Broadley, Jimmy Butcher, Colum Cameron, Jonathan Cleaver, Dan Dixon, Amy Drummond, Andrew Dunn, Molly Garnier, Rebecca Gerrard, Dawid Grudzinski, Linda Gunn, Robyn Hardy, Zophie Horsted, Neil Johnstone, Kate Leiper, Dane Lord, Heather Marshall, Ailsa McLaggan, Adam Millar, John Mitchell, Tom Nickson, Christie O'Carroll, Amanda Olson, Clare Padgett, Finlay Pretsell, Greg Sinclair, Corin Sluggett, Emma Taylor, Gillian Taylor, Ailsa Thomson, Matt Vale, Matthew Ward, Jenna Watt, Kris Wedlock, Katie Wilson.

Traverse Theatre Board of Directors: Stephen Cotton (Chair), Roy Campbell, Leslie Evans, Chris Hannan, Christine Hamilton, Caroline Gardner, John Stone, Stuart Murray (Company Secretary), Margaret Waterston.

MELODY

First published in 2006 by Oberon Books Ltd

521 Caledonian Road, London N7 9RH

Tel: 020 7607 3637 / Fax: 020 7607 3629

e-mail: info@oberonbooks.com

www.oberonbooks.com

A catalogue record for this book is available from the British Library.

ISBN: 1 84002 663 4

Cover photograph by Euan Myles

Printed in Great Britain by Antony Rowe Ltd, Chippenham

For my family

Characters

MELODY (38)
JOHN (19)
OLIVE (70)
ASHLEY (19)

1

It's about 5.30 in the evening. The living room of a wee house, with a tiny kitchen/breakfast bar. There is a front door. Beyond that: the sea. There is a window which, if it were not dark with rain, would have a fairly unspectacular view. Another door leads offstage into the other rooms of the house. The house itself looks shaky – like a holiday chalet. It's a house which could never look pristine no matter how hard you tried. But someone obviously does. The furniture is mixed and matched, old and poor, but optimistically covered in throws, and there are traces of real effort: a vase, flowers, stencils on the woodchip. The house has a determined woman's touch. But it's fighting a losing battle.

A large PC on a specially-built PC desk is stuffed in the corner and is surrounded by IT debris. There is an old TV in the other corner. It is being kept alive in the modern world by a host of attachments – DVD/Playstation 2, etc – like an old man in a hospital.

This is MELODY's house and she's happy with it.

She's in her late thirties and is sitting on the couch wearing a bright yellow polo shirt which has the word 'Munchies' on the chest. It's her uniform from work. She is also wearing a white, long-sleeved T-shirt underneath, covering her arms.

JOHN is 19. He is wearing a white shirt with a name badge on it, sleeves rolled up, collar open and slippers. He still has traces of acne.

Sitting forgotten in her usual chair is OLIVE. She's an old lady and she looks, to the casual observer, to be 100% dead. An untouched china tea cup and biscuit is on her side table. Her eyes are closed, her mouth gaping, her arms wide, palms out as if she were the star of a strange religious picture. No breathing movements, no whispers from the other two. Invisible for the moment.

JOHN stands in front of MELODY. He's in the middle of something. MELODY's videoing him on a mobile phone.

JOHN: I put it to you that you're nothing but a liar! A fake! Pretending to be someone you're not! A dirty, sneaky, tricky wee...em... There's a word but I can't think of it now. I want to say dobber...

MELODY: Say dobber then.

JOHN: Dobber. Nah that's unprofessional.

MELODY: Cut?

JOHN: No! Keep rolling. The viewers have to see this.

MELODY: Well... I think the...

Phone's run out of video time.

JOHN: Keep rolling. We'll edit it. You've lied to the House of Commons and you're lying to my viewers now. Answer the question! Answer the question! Why won't you answer the question? Is it because, in fact, the aliens are already here, kidding on to be high ranking politicians so they can destroy the human race as we know it? And you, *you* Prime Minister, are their egg-bearing Queen? How do you plead? How do you plead? And we'll freeze it there. Close up. Let the viewers draw their own conclusions. And that's it. The most famous interview ever. Beamed around the world. Wee guys watching in Africa, tramps outside Comet, the works. What do you reckon?

MELODY: Oh it's...

JOHN: Penetrating.

MELODY: I think it's penetrating. Fantastic.

JOHN: I was nearly away there man. Honestly, I had to hold it in. This is the one. Think about it right, how many audition tapes will they get?

MELODY: Hundreds.

JOHN: Millions probably. But how many will show someone un-veiling the Prime Minister as the egg-bearing Queen of an alien race? Hardly any.

MELODY: I know. Super. I'm not sure it all taped though John.

JOHN: Eh? There's three minutes on that.

MELODY: I know but it just froze.

JOHN: Ach you've probably stopped it with your great big thumbs. Well we'll have to do a re-shoot.

MELODY: Great big thumbs! Where's that come from? My thumbs are perfectly normal.

JOHN: They're unprofessional. Right, start again.

MELODY: Naw. Cheeky swine. I'm out of here in ten minutes anyway. We'll do it later.

JOHN: But I'm in the zone now!

MELODY: Well good for you, but I've got to work. You can get in the zone again when I get back.

JOHN: The zone'll be gone by then. Ach, you've ruined now. And I've got my CV here all ready to go 'n all. You were going to check it.

MELODY sighs and looks a bit lost. She then pulls a strange, overly cheerful face which seems to give her a boost and the energy to carry on.

MELODY: Let's see it then. Wow. This is ace baby. No mistakes. It's…you were in the majorettes?

JOHN: Not for long.

MELODY: You kept that quiet. Super. Can I pin it to the fridge?

JOHN: No! It's a…this is a professional thingby…a professional CV. You cannae…tch. Pin it to the fridge! How would it stay up?

MELODY: I'll force it in with my great big unprofessional thumb. How do you think, magnets.

JOHN: Well. Alright.

She pins it up. Gives it a wee round of applause.

MELODY: When's the deadline for the competition?

JOHN: Friday.

MELODY: Oh God then, you'll need to get a move on.

JOHN: How?

MELODY: Sending it away.

JOHN: I'm not sending it away.

MELODY: Why?

JOHN: I live in a paperless world that's why. I'll bung it on the website with my CV. It'll intrigue them.

MELODY: But what if they don't go to your website?

JOHN: I've sent them the link. The word is out.

MELODY: Would it not be easier just to send it in normally?

JOHN: It's a professional touch. It's intriguing.

MELODY: But what if they can't be bothered?

JOHN: They're intrigued!

MELODY: But…

JOHN: Melody!

MELODY: Yeah okay, okay. Sorry doll. Just…and do you think when they said they wanted a video of you interviewing someone that they maybe meant somebody real?

JOHN: The Prime Minister's real.

MELODY: Aye...but...

JOHN: Who else am I going to interview? You? Aye right.

MELODY: That's not very nice John. If you're so bored you can move all your stuff back over the road to your mum's. I'm starting to see why she chucked you out ya wee brat.

JOHN: She's not my mum. And she didn't chuck me out. I left. I'm a grown man.

MELODY: Aye right baby face. A grown man? What makes you say that?

JOHN: Well look where I am.

MELODY: So?

JOHN: Babies don't live with people do they?

MELODY: Aye. Their mums.

JOHN: I hate her.

MELODY: She was upset. People get upset when you take them for granted and act like a brat.

JOHN: You made that soup as a peace offering and she threw it back in your face. That's assault.

MELODY: I'm not talking about that. You just called me boring. I want an apology.

JOHN: You could've been scalded.

MELODY: John!

JOHN: Alright. Sorry Melody. I didn't mean it. You *are* interesting hen. When you were in the band and all that. More interesting than me anyroads.

MELODY: Aye okay. Thank you. But you're interesting too babe.

JOHN: I will be if I win this competition. That'll be it started. Big time.

MELODY: That'll be what started?

JOHN: My life.

MELODY: Aye. I suppose it will. You're right anyway, what do I know? Send in what you want. You're the presenter. It's your adventure. I'm just the waitress stroke petrol station attendant. (*She makes that smiling face again.*) I'm like a super hero. Mild-mannered waitress during the day, but by night she becomes...a mild-mannered petrol station attendant! Nice day at work?

JOHN: Well I'm just about to show you. You see, unlike *some*, I update the diary on my web page so that interested parties can find out things at any time, day or night, wherever they are in the world.

MELODY: When did you update it?

JOHN: Today at the shop. Hacked into Henry's dad's wireless.

MELODY: Does Henry's dad not mind you hacking into his wireless?

JOHN: Henry's dad's a cock. When was the last time you updated *your* website by the way?

MELODY: Em...well...

JOHN: Ach Melody. What's the point in having a website if you don't update it? I've got half a mind to take you off my links.

MELODY: Ooooh, I'm scared. What would happen if you took me off your links John? Death? Anyway, who's going to go to my website? Some middle-aged stalker with a thumb fetish?

JOHN: It's just a weekly diary. Wouldn't kill you to change it once in a while.

MELODY: I know. I should. Change the dates.

JOHN: Change the words too that's the point. And you could check your e-mails 'n aw. I sent you a picture of a baby with Olive's face grafted on to it weeks ago, and what thanks do I get? None. I mean, it took me ages to build you a site, it's the least you could do to check your bloody e-mails.

MELODY: I know. I know. I'm horrible amint I? I will. What's the time? I'd better get changed. I'm so tired.

MELODY exits.

(*Off.*) Are you remembering that the girl from Home Help might be popping round tonight? Either tonight or tomorrow. John? She's young Maggie says.

JOHN: Aye but Maggie also says that Jesus is coming back in October to breathe fire and shoot lightning at The Magnum. Not exactly a reliable source of information know what I mean. Here we are look.

MELODY enters wearing a different uniform. This time it's for a petrol station.

MELODY: Aye it's a shame. There was me saying she was out the other end of that breakdown as well. Then wee Charles goes and gets an ASBO and it's back to square one with the fire-breathing Jesus stuff. Just goes to show you. Ach everything'll be alright. Keep a cheery face.

JOHN: Diary. Double click. 'Wednesday. Fixed PC for the Hoover Shop. Practised interview which is penetrating.

Henry's dad made sarcastic remark about me fannying about. Made diary entry on website.' That's it. See. If you want to know how my day was you can find out just like that.

MELODY: Amazing. You're amazing you know that. Give us some sugar. (*They kiss.*) You going to be alright with Olive tonight?

JOHN: Aye. I've got the Witchfinder General coming round. She's going to have a bath.

MELODY: Ach away, that's a sin.

JOHN: She's a sin.

MELODY: Sssh you'll wake her up.

JOHN: Wake her up? She *is* awake. She's kidding on to sleep just to listen to us talking. Horrible old…

MELODY: She looks asleep.

JOHN: Well she's not. She's just preserving her energy for her next wild accusation.

MELODY: In fact she looks…a wee bit dead.

JOHN: Accusing folk of stuff they've not done. I never done it Mel. I could sue her. She's going the right way to get sued, if she keeps on accusing folk of that kind of thing.

MELODY: John soosh a minute. Doesn't she look a wee bit dead to you?

JOHN: She's not dead. If she was dead, Satan's minions would've been at the door looking to drag her down to her new residence. Aye, she'll no be complaining about the cold tea down there.

MELODY: I mean it! Is she breathing?

JOHN: Get a mirror.

MELODY: To check her breath?

JOHN: I was going to say to fix your hair, but I suppose… Ahya. Stop punching me!

MELODY: (*Leaving to the bedroom.*) Well grow up then.

She's gone.

JOHN: (*Beat. To OLIVE.*) You're awake. I know you're awake. See. I can see that you're awake. Oh I know you're awake. You're not dead, ya…bloody…accuser. Accusing people. Now the tables have turned. *I'm* accusing *you*. I'm accusing you of not being dead. How do ye like that eh ya horrible old…?

Enter MELODY at pace with a hand mirror.

MELODY: I'm gonna have to watch my time here.

MELODY kneels down beside OLIVE and holds a mirror under her nose and mouth testing for her breath.

JOHN: What time you back?

MELODY: About nine. It's not a full shift. Come on Olive breathe.

JOHN: And what about the cleaner?

MELODY: She's not a cleaner. She's a home help. Just be polite to her. She's just testing us tonight, see if we're nice, then it's every Tuesday. It might even be tomorrow she comes Maggie says. Oh God John…

JOHN: What?

MELODY: She's not breathing.

JOHN: Aye she is.

MELODY: She isnae. Look (*Holds out the mirror.*) Oh God! Olive's dead.

JOHN: She isnae. She'll be holding her breath.

MELODY: Oh God. What are we going to do? John?

JOHN: Fiver she's holding her breath.

MELODY: What do we do? What if it was…they'll say that I…

JOHN: Wait.

MELODY: But…

JOHN: Wait.

> *JOHN holds out his hand and MELODY waits, all eyes on OLIVE. A big beat. Then…OLIVE wakes up gasping for air and leaning forward. She immediately turns this gasp into a very unconvincing yawn.*

OLIVE: Oh. I was dreaming Francis had returned, God bless his soul. Tea'll be cold is it?

JOHN: Ha! Thank you very much. That'll be a fiver.

MELODY: Ach Olive you had us worried there.

OLIVE: For yourself. Yes, yes. Cold as ice.

MELODY: You shouldn't do that Olive.

OLIVE: Do what? Sleep? Oh I shouldn't sleep now is that it? Mind you, I suppose it's only fair. I get no food, just enough cigarettes to keep me alive, cold tea, and now I've to have the further delight of sleep deprivation. Wonderful! Oh the punishments one must suffer in the evening of one's life for that distant morning of pleasure.

MELODY: Do you want fresh tea? John'll do it, I'm nearly away.

> *He doesn't, so during the following MELODY has to make the tea herself.*

OLIVE: And I wonder what I would see if I did bow down to you and stay awake all night? What *images* would I be forced to behold in the dark?

JOHN: Here we go.

OLIVE: A woman of my age. A respected and adored woman in her youth…

MELODY: Your new home help's coming for a visit later maybe. So be nice. She's young Maggie says.

OLIVE: Can hardly walk. My moonlit dancing days long gone. There I am, hobbling, quite unaided, for a glass of water in the middle of the night, so desperate for any moisture am I, and what did I see? And what did I see? What hellish vision appeared to me? At two in the morning!

JOHN: Hobbling my arse! She practically ran in. She was like Lara Croft bounding in. I shat myself.

MELODY: John.

OLIVE: Him…sitting at that thing…naked from the waist down!!

JOHN: I wasn't fucking doing anything!!

MELODY: JOHN!

OLIVE: Oh yes, the wonderful language of a self abuser. In the gutter. I'm to die in the gutter with strangers. Forced to stay awake all night watching dirty boys dirtying themselves.

JOHN: For the last time you spying old cow, I was updating my iPod.

OLIVE: He admits it!

MELODY: Please. The pair of you. John. Don't speak like that to Olive, she's been to the Queen's Garden Party. Show some respect. That computer can go back.

OLIVE: He's more than likely a rapist.

MELODY: No. He's not Olive. That's a terrible thing to say. Now you've had all your cigarettes today am I right?

OLIVE: No! I've one more. One more Melody.

MELODY: Well we'll see.

OLIVE: No! I've got one more. I have.

MELODY: Well. We'll see. When I get back. So stop calling him a rapist, men are touchy about that.

OLIVE: Yes. Alright. But I have one more. (*Louder.*) And I know all about men. In my youth I became an expert as they fluttered like moths to my flame. And unlike you I've had a son, so I know all about *boys* too. Francis, God bless his soul. Oh Melody, what did you do to send him away? You must be devastated to have lost Francis and get stuck with…*him.*

MELODY: (*To JOHN and barely audible.*) I don't want Francis I want you.

JOHN: I don't care.

MELODY: 'The night-times of the past are best forgotten by day.'

JOHN: I don't care.

MELODY: Right. I'm…oh God look at the rain. Do you think the sea's going to come over the wall? Should we get some sandbags from somewhere?

JOHN: Sandbags?

MELODY: In case we get flooded.

JOHN: Aye but sandbags don't work. Every time you see folk flooded on the TV they've always got sandbags, but they're still flooded. Sandbags! That's the beach over there Melody. That's all the sand you could want. Digging it up and stuffing it into bags isnae gonna help.

MELODY: Okay, don't get out your pram. Just don't want you getting swept away before your big competition. You should read his CV Olive, it's very good.

OLIVE: Pfft! TV presenter! The fact that he aspires to be like those grinning cretins should tell you all you need to know about the depth of his character. Aliens and Prime Ministers! It's nonsensical gibberish. I don't need to read anything to tell you that. Before my eyes went I read voraciously. Devoured the classics. I read *A Tale of Two Cities* to Francis before he could walk.

JOHN: That's probably *why* he learned to walk. So he could get away from you bloody boring him.

OLIVE: That's why Francis was an artist! A genius child. God bless his soul.

JOHN: Wait a minute. How do you know my interview's got aliens and Prime Ministers in it if you were sleeping? Eh?

OLIVE: Ach, they've all got daft aliens in them all your daft things.

JOHN: Aye but they've no all got Prime Ministers in them. See! She *was* spying.

OLIVE: Well he *was* abusing himself. I can prove it.

JOHN: How can you prove it?

OLIVE: I need my glasses. Melody? Glasses?

MELODY: They'll be down the side of your chair Olive. (*Putting OLIVE's tea next to her.*) Right folks, I'm away.

Try not to kill each other if the home help comes. And please pretend to be normal. Bye bye. I…

OLIVE: Wait! Where?

MELODY gets the glasses out from down the side of chair. OLIVE puts them on and produces a tiny folded-up bit of newspaper which she unfolds so slowly and grandly that MELODY waits to see what it is.

'There are many readers who share your worries about pornography on the internet. Although many men who are addicted believe they can escape detection by wiping the history from their server, this does *not* mean all traces have been removed. The past is always traceable. Open a DOS folder, click on CD. Open Temporary…' and it goes on. It's all there. *You* can have it Melody and I want you to follow the instructions and discover what filth and immorality *he* feasts on while you and I sleep.

MELODY: (*Taking the clipping.*) Lovely. Right I'm off. This time. I love you both.

JOHN: Right.

OLIVE: This tea's cold.

MELODY opens the door to leave but is immediately greeted by ASHLEY.

MELODY: Oh! What a fright. Perfect timing.

ASHLEY: Here is your fear…

MELODY: (*Not listening and interrupting.*) Come in, come in. I'm late for my shift but John'll make you a wee cup of tea.

OLIVE: Two! And boil it!

ASHLEY: Here is your fear……

MELODY: This is John. (*To OLIVE.*) You'll help her won't you?

OLIVE: (*Waves her hands as if dismissing a servant.*) Pfft!

MELODY: She's lovely. I'm so sorry about me not being here. Very unprofessional. Help yourself to whatever. Right that's me away.

And she's gone.

OLIVE: I won't let you do laundry. You can do dishes, cleaning and if you make soup, you can make soup. Otherwise don't. I don't like organic food. Or anything greasy. In my youth I drank champagne from oyster shells whilst watching falling stars from the edge of a jetty. Those days are over.

ASHLEY: (*To OLIVE.*) It's not you is it?

JOHN: Aye it's her. You might get lucky and she'll be sleeping but watch because sometimes she fakes it. Ha ha h...mmm.

ASHLEY: (*To OLIVE.*) Are you Melody Moore?

OLIVE: Pfft!

JOHN: Oh right, naw she's Olive. That was Melody.

ASHLEY looks at JOHN as if he's deliberately messed up her life.

ASHLEY: Fuck sake!

ASHLEY goes out the door after MELODY but she's gone. ASHLEY re-enters. She goes to the window.

OLIVE: Here you! You'll clean your mouth out. I've a good mind to get on to Maggie and you'll be out that door. Everything has to be filth.

JOHN: Ach ignore her. You can swear all you want.

31

ASHLEY: Fuck!

ASHLEY's on her mobile phone.

JOHN: Yeah. Fuck. Shit. You name it. Arsehole. Fanny. Well not fanny. Unless you want to… I mean it's up to you. I wouldn't……so…anything. Em… I'm John by the way. I'm in charge.

OLIVE: Aye, like you were in charge of that barbecue?

JOHN: That's…that's got absolutely nothing to do with anything. Why would you…?

ASHLEY holds out her finger and JOHN is silenced.

ASHLEY: (*To the phone.*) Where are you? (*She goes to the window.*) You're not… Where?… I can't see you…Well she's…no that's what I'm saying she's gone… I don't know but she…no I saw her walk straight out…Well maybe that's how she's going to play it…

JOHN: (*To OLIVE.*) Maggie.

ASHLEY: There's a boy with the old woman… (*To JOHN.*) …who are you?

JOHN: John.

ASHLEY: John… I don't know…kind of fat. Baby face… (*To JOHN.*) …are you Melody's son?

OLIVE spins round and laughs for a long, long time. She finally stops. And then turns back into her huff position.

JOHN: No. Me and her are…kind of…you know what I mean. I live here and everything.

ASHLEY: (*To phone.*) He lives here and everything…are you fucking her?

OLIVE: Eh?!

JOHN: (*To OLIVE, explaining.*) It's Maggie. She's off the rails. Wee Charles is a lesbo now or something and it's put her back to the old… (*Mimes a fire-breathing Jesus.*)

OLIVE: For God sake.

JOHN: Tell her it's John the boyfriend. From the computer shop.

ASHLEY: Boyfriend… but why… (*To JOHN.*) When will Mrs Robinson be back?

JOHN: Eh?

ASHLEY: (*Covering the phone.*) Chill. My lover's an older man who like totally opened my cage. He's a radical artist who expresses himself through sex and his own therapy techniques.

JOHN: He sounds nice.

ASHLEY: He's not. He believes only in confrontation. But his age, experience and emotional anarchy have allowed me to express myself realistically whilst I'm expunging all the toxins of the past.

JOHN: Oh well. Very good.

ASHLEY: When will she be back? Melody?

JOHN: Dunno. About nine or something. Do you want a cup of tea?

OLIVE: Two! Boil it!

JOHN goes about making the tea.

ASHLEY: (*Back on the phone.*) About nine or something… But why can't I wait in the car with you?…but he's… what, instead of her?…should I give him the envelope… oh I see…but… (*Quietly.*) … I've not practised anything for him… I don't know if I can… (*On the other end of the phone the voice is giving her a long pep talk that has an*

immediate effect. She straightens up and fills with courage.
She eyes JOHN malevolently.) ...really?...really?... God
you're... I will... I know...everything must go tonight.
(*Suddenly a love-struck teenager.*) You're so fucking
beautiful it's untrue!!!... Forever. (*She hangs up, drops the*
smile and instantly turns into a completely in control woman
on a mission.)

OLIVE: You look too young.

ASHLEY: I'm nineteen.

OLIVE: I won't let you anywhere near an iron if that's
what you're thinking.

ASHLEY: She's got balls I'll give her that.

JOHN: Who Maggie? Wouldnae surprise me.

ASHLEY: To just blank us. To pretend this isn't
happening, that takes balls. I admire her. She's even got
you two well trained. Very impressive. Not replying was
one thing...but this, leaving me alone in her Oedipal
nest.

JOHN: (*Laughs.*) Yeah.

OLIVE: He doesn't understand. He thinks *Oedipus Rex* is a
dinosaur. Ha! Don't be fooled by the tea making by the
way. He's up all night abusing himself on that thing.

JOHN: Shut your face you!

OLIVE: He's a rapist.

JOHN: I'm telling Melody and you know what'll happen.
No more purple haze daytripping.

OLIVE: Child.

JOHN finishes off the teas and hands them out with varying
degrees of courtesy.

JOHN: She doesn't understand computers. I do. She's out of her depth in the modern world.

OLIVE: Pfft.

JOHN: Do you want to see my website?

OLIVE: (*Whispers to ASHLEY.*) Here. Open a DOS, click a CD……

OLIVE makes a 'we'll finish this later' gesture.

ASHLEY: Okay. I'll bite. If this is your first move, so be it.

JOHN: Yeah. And if you click here it goes to diary. Or it should. Come on!

ASHLEY: That says dairy.

JOHN: It's under construction.

ASHLEY: Who's that?

JOHN: That, is a picture of me with Eamonn Holmes. You can't really see me cos of Melody's thumb but I'm there. You can just make out my can of Fanta.

ASHLEY: Who's Eamonn Holmes?

JOHN: Who's Eamonn Holmes? Aye right. He's very impressive up close. He always keeps his cool. Keeps his head. Very professional. I was impressed.

ASHLEY: He looks a bit pissed off.

JOHN: Well you'd be pissed off too if someone had just spilt Fanta all over you just before a live broadcast. But to his credit, he never mentioned it and let the viewers draw their own conclusions. He shook my hand afterwards. Totally inspired me. I'm going to be a TV presenter. Not so much like Eamonn, more, you know, penetrating. I'm very professional. I've got a CV and everything.

ASHLEY: You're not kidding are you? TV presenter. Yeah. Yeah. Okay. That might… (*To OLIVE, shaking her head.*) I expected better than this, I've got to tell you. Easy. She's really not prepared you at all. (*Back to JOHN.*) Can I see it? Your CV?

JOHN: It's on the fridge.

ASHLEY: (*Reading the CV.*) You see the reason I'm interested is…you were in the majorettes?

JOHN: Not for long.

ASHLEY: No…em…the reason I'm interested is that I actually know a lot of people in television. High up in television actually. Yeah. Daddy's friends. Well, they'd do anything for me. I think I could like, really pull some strings. You know what I mean?

JOHN: Really?

ASHLEY: Really.

JOHN: Well…why?

ASHLEY: I dunno. I have a feeling about you John. Of course I'd need to see you doing your stuff first…

OLIVE: He doesn't want it really. He just wants to put it into his daft computer and pretend.

ASHLEY: Is that true John?

JOHN: No.

ASHLEY: Cos I have to know you're for real if I'm going to do this.

JOHN: I'm for real. She just…don't listen to her. I've already got half of an interview on a phone. It's controversial.

OLIVE: It's nonsensical.

JOHN: It's not for everyone. I could do a live interview though. Like, you know, interview you or something.

ASHLEY: Are you asking me out on a date?

JOHN: NO! I mean. Here. Now. Or never. Maybe. You know, jeezo, c'mon, water under the...we could just... you know. How's the tea?

ASHLEY: Okay Eamonn relax. It's a nice idea. We could do an interview. Cool. They really respect my opinions back at HQ.

JOHN: So do I. 100%.

ASHLEY: And it'll kill some time before old Melody gets back. Where is she anyway? Where has she fled to?

JOHN: Glendoune Garage. She works there at night. She's saving up to have her tattoos removed. Ugly bloody things. They're from her Rock 'n Roll days.

OLIVE: Rockabilly.

JOHN: Rockabilly. I hate tattoos.

ASHLEY: I've got tattoos.

JOHN: Some are nice though. Some are very nice. Hers are horrible.

OLIVE: I wonder why you think they're horrible?

JOHN: Shut up.

OLIVE: When is it she's getting *your* name tattooed all over her? Oh yes now I remember. Never. (*Has a sip of tea.*) Ach for God sake! I think there's something wrong with that kettle. Either that or you're just inept.

ASHLEY puts her hand on his shoulder. At first he jumps but she keeps her hand there. Brushing his neck. JOHN lets her. He's terrified/turned on.

ASHLEY: I wonder how else we're alike? Me and Melody I mean? You'll need to compare and contrast us, eh John? Check out my tattoos. Phil designed them. He's like an amazing artist.

JOHN: Does he work for the home help folk?

ASHLEY: No. The establishment can't handle his radical ideas so at the minute he's a postman. He literally knocked on my door and changed my life. He's the reason I'm here. He came up with the entire plan. He found the proof, he sent the e-mails, everything. He gave me a future. He opened my cage. Maybe I could do the same for you?

ASHLEY slips her hand down the back of JOHN's shirt. He's rigid, frozen, eyes straight ahead. OLIVE's pretending not to see.

JOHN: So...em...do you think you'll take it right enough?

ASHLEY: Oh I'll take it all right. I'll take it all. I have to or I'll be stuck in the past forever. If Phil's taught me anything he's taught me that tonight, everything must go.

JOHN: Good. I mean... I'll bet you're good at it. Probably.

ASHLEY: How did you know?

JOHN: Good at the job! *This* job I mean! Not...you know...you look...you know...

ASHLEY: How do I look John?

JOHN: You look...good.

ASHLEY: Oh really?

JOHN: At cleaning I mean. You look like a top of the range cleaner. No offence. Cos you're nothing like a cleaner in many ways. Even though, essentially, you are a cleaner.

OLIVE: She's not a cleaner.

ASHLEY: I'm not a cleaner.

OLIVE: She's a home help.

ASHLEY: I'm not a home help either.

OLIVE: Well I don't know what you call them. Caregiver. Maggie was happy with home help until she took her breakdown and so should you be.

ASHLEY: But I'm not a home help.

JOHN: Aye but it was Maggie that sent you eh?

ASHLEY: No.

OLIVE: So who sent you?

ASHLEY takes her hands off JOHN.

ASHLEY: Yeah right. You've been dreading this moment.

Blank looks exchanged between OLIVE and JOHN.

That's why she fled. I can't believe it either, but that's how she's chosen to play it. Leaving you two wide open. (*To OLIVE.*) And you, just letting me get into him, very clever. (*To JOHN.*) In case you haven't noticed, we're playing a dangerous game of cat and mouse here.

JOHN: First I've heard of it.

ASHLEY: What?

JOHN: What you on about?

ASHLEY: Fuck sake. She's mentioned the e-mails though? Tell me she's mentioned the fucking e-mails. The e-mails! We've been sending ten e-mails a day. The abusive e-mails? It's a hate campaign. I can't *believe* she hasn't mentioned it.

JOHN: Ach she doesnae check her e-mails. I keep telling her: you should check your bloody e-mails!

OLIVE: Tell me this then. If you're not a home help what do you do?

ASHLEY: I'm a suicide bomber. I'm here to blow you all apart. That's what the messages said. I expected you to know this. 'Here is your fear. I'm here to destroy you.' Ring any bells? It was a countdown. It started weeks ago. Counting down to this. Tonight is the night Melody has to face her past. To pay for her crime. It's all about… (*Pulls out an envelope.*) …this. I'm here to rip her life to pieces. It's fucking basic stuff!

OLIVE: Suicide bombers. I told you Maggie would end up as a suicide bomber. That's how it always starts, fire-breathing Jesuses.

ASHLEY: I don't know anyone called fucking Maggie!

JOHN: Where's your bomb then?

ASHLEY: I don't have a fucking bomb! It's a fucking metaphor! By destroying Melody and her fake ideas of the past I destroy my old self too so I can move on. You see? It's not fucking complicated! His phone's off. I can't believe she doesn't check her fucking e-mails. Who doesn't check their fucking e-mails? Phil said she would check her e-mails. Where is he?

JOHN: Ach it's a nightmare. She says she cannae understand it, but I take her through it step by step. Go into Outlook Express, double click on the…

OLIVE: QUIET! Quiet. Who are you then? Who are you really?

Pause. The quiet gives ASHLEY back some of her power.

ASHLEY: I'm Ashley. I'm Ashley Brown.

A tick-tock, tick-tock pause as both OLIVE and JOHN search to see if that name should mean something to them. JOHN draws a complete blank and looks to OLIVE. Nothing at first. Then...

OLIVE: AAAAAAAAAAHHHHHHHHHH!!!!!!!!!!!shly Brown!

Half a beat for a big breath and then in panic, and with no forethought, OLIVE throws her tea in JOHN's face. Down he goes...

JOHN: Aaaaargh!!!!

Blackout as JOHN hits the carpet.

2

Some time has passed. JOHN lies on the couch with a cloth over his face, head on ASHLEY's lap, quietly moaning. ASHLEY is nursing him and stroking him sensually. OLIVE is nowhere to be seen. MELODY enters from outside looking absolutely delighted. She bounds in, not really taking in the scene, whips off her coat and throws her arms out triumphantly.

MELODY: Yeeess!!! Guess what? I forgot I'd swapped with Tina so she could go to Alan's golf do on Saturday. I walked in there and Tina's like that 'What are you doing here?' I wrote it on the calendar as well look. She's like that 'You're a dozy moo'. Ya absolute beauty. I love it. It's like when you forget it's a Saturday. (*Finally she has spotted that something's not quite right. To ASHLEY.*) Oh Hiya. Still here. Where's… Ah! Oh my God what is it? What's he done to Olive?

JOHN bolts up on the couch but keeps the cloth over his face. He shouts from under it as if it's a veil.

JOHN: What have *I* done to *her*? I've done nothing to her. What's she done to me you should be asking.

MELODY: Oh God. What has she done?

JOHN: Scalded me beyond all recognition. That's what she's done.

MELODY: Oh my God.

JOHN: I tell you Melody I've never felt pain like it. I never want to go through that again.

MELODY goes to cuddle him but ASHLEY pulls him even closer. MELODY feels a tiny something but lets it go.

MELODY: Aw baby. This is terrible.

MELODY mouths 'Where's Olive?' to ASHLEY. ASHLEY smiles and points off to the bedrooms etc. MELODY nods.

JOHN: No! Don't look at me!

MELODY: Is it bad?

JOHN: I'll show you Melody, but you've to promise not to get frightened.

MELODY: Okay.

JOHN: Okay.

> *JOHN very slowly, and very dramatically unveils himself. There is, of course, nothing wrong with his face, except it's tear-stained and screwed up as if he's being tortured. MELODY looks closely. Her worry gives way to annoyance. She punches him on the arm.*

MELODY: Ach see you! You had me totally worried there ya big baby. There's nothing bloody wrong with you.

JOHN: Eh?

MELODY: There's nothing wrong with you, you're fine. (*To ASHLEY.*) What happened?

ASHLEY: Tea was thrown.

JOHN: Give me the mirror a minute.

MELODY: Tea was thrown?

JOHN: What are you talking about, it's totally red. Look.

MELODY: It is not. Why was tea thrown?

OLIVE: (*Off and scared.*) It was an accident. Melody can I have a word?

JOHN: An accident! How was it an accident ya old cow? After she screamed right, there was about three seconds, 1, 2, 3, then whoosh she chucked it straight at me. It was a clear chuck.

> *OLIVE appears, poking her head round the corner of the living room meekly.*

OLIVE: I was seized by the air of panic in the room.

MELODY: Why was there an air of panic in the room? Why were people screaming?

JOHN: You took *advantage* of the air of panic, thought to yourself 'Ya dancer, here's my chance to scald the wee prick' and *clearly* chucked the tea. She's been wanting to scald me since the day I moved in here.

OLIVE: Oh grow up. Even if I did, you couldn't scald anyone with the tea you get in this house.

MELODY: (*To ASHLEY.*) God you must think we're all mad. It's not normally like this. Well tea's never been thrown before. I can't understand it.

ASHLEY: Of course not.

OLIVE: Melody.

ASHLEY: So I'll enlighten you. It was an instinct. She was lashing out at a force she can't understand.

OLIVE: Melody!

ASHLEY: She knew she couldn't fight it so she attacked the person below her in the food chain, offering him up in the hope she'll be spared. But you wouldn't understand that Melody, you wouldn't understand anything, because you…*you*…do not check your e-mails!

JOHN: I told you.

ASHLEY: And when Phil hears about that he's going to be very upset. He went to a lot of trouble you know. He would lie awake at night worrying about the wording.

MELODY: Is Phil the new Maggie?

JOHN: She doesnae know Maggie.

OLIVE: Melody!

JOHN: She's a suicide bomber.

OLIVE: MELODY!!!!!! CAN I TALK TO YOU!!!!!!

MELODY: God sake Olive hen what's wrong? Just speak. What's going on? Tell me.

OLIVE: Away from them. Away from her. Whatever she is.

MELODY: Alright. Jeezo. I've only been away five minutes and the whole place goes nuts. Oh well. (*Puts on her cheery face. It doesn't quite take. She can't suss this out.*) It's a madhouse. Two ticks.

OLIVE scuttles off and MELODY follows, giving just the tiny flicker of a glance over her shoulder at JOHN snuggled up in ASHLEY's arms.

ASHLEY: How's your face?

JOHN: Agony.

ASHLEY: You can like totally see a mark.

JOHN: I know. She thinks I exaggerate about stuff. She treats me like a...fucking...wee...

ASHLEY: Prick.

JOHN: Aye. I'm a total victim man.

ASHLEY: There's something about scalding that really appeals to me. Scorching off the layers of skin until the bitter raw redness of flesh is left stinging in the air. The truth at last. You know what I mean?

JOHN sucks air through his teeth in pain and feels his face.

Have you ever used fire during sex?

JOHN: Eh?

ASHLEY: Dripping wax, hot pokers, branding irons?

JOHN: Eh?

ASHLEY: There's something primeval about fire. Goes right back to our animal origins. Just like sex. They go well together.

JOHN: Nah… I…just…it's…nah.

ASHLEY: Do you and Melody go well together?

JOHN: Aye.

ASHLEY: Do you think she'll cry when you…

JOHN: What?

ASHLEY: Leave.

JOHN: But I won't leave.

ASHLEY: You'll have to. When you get work as a presenter.

JOHN: Was that…*real* then?

ASHLEY: Of course baby. Don't you believe me?

JOHN: Yeah. Well. I'd come back though. At night.

ASHLEY: From London? You know this is only temporary here don't you? You want out.

JOHN: I don't though.

ASHLEY: I thought you said you were serious about this?

JOHN: I am.

ASHLEY: Well be honest then. You've got like, a burning talent John. A talent that's going to take you all around the world. People here just want to hold you back. You can't let them. I was a prisoner once. I know how it feels. Your cage is about to be opened and your new life is just about to start. Don't fuck it up. You'll have new clothes, new lovers, new name…

JOHN: New name?

ASHLEY: Of course. All presenters have stage names.

JOHN: I wouldnae mind that. See me right, when I was adopted, they didnae name me for a year. They just called me Baby. For a whole year. They wanted to give me a name that suited my personality! And do you know what they decided on after a year?

ASHLEY: No.

JOHN: Aye you do. John. John! A year and that's what they come up with. Bastards.

ASHLEY: Yeah that's what I'm…

JOHN: I hate my mum. She threw soup at Melody.

ASHLEY: John concentrate.

JOHN: She says I'll make a fool of myself on TV. That's why I'm doing this. There was another time right…

ASHLEY: John. Quiet. Focus. This is what I'm trying to tell you. You're better than these old losers. You need to be with young people. Have you ever even had sex with a girl your own age?

JOHN: I dunno.

ASHLEY: You don't know?

JOHN: Aye. Just…

ASHLEY: You haven't have you? Melody's your first. Is that why you stay with her? Because she lets you and no-one else will? You must wonder though. What young skin feels like. Firm breasts in your fingers. Flat smooth stomach under yours. Tight ass clenching with every thrust. Hard tanned thighs tight around your hips. Have you got a hard on?

JOHN tries to get up. ASHLEY wraps her legs around him. Trapping him, groin to groin, although if he really tried he could easily escape.

JOHN: What are you doing?

ASHLEY: You're very attractive.

JOHN: I am not! What you doing?

ASHLEY: I can feel you. I can feel that you want me to get you out of here.

JOHN: Can you? But…it can be nice here, sometimes.

ASHLEY: What? Sitting in every night in your slippers drinking tea?

JOHN: Aye.

ASHLEY: With an old tattooed slapper treating you like a baby?

JOHN: She's not a slapper. She's kind.

ASHLEY: Kind? Wow. Sexy.

JOHN: She is kind. I want her.

ASHLEY: More than you want me to make you a famous TV presenter? More than you want me to fuck you.

JOHN: I don't want you to…

ASHLEY: That's not what I can feel.

JOHN: Leave me alone.

ASHLEY loosens her grip on JOHN but he stays in place. Pause.

ASHLEY: I'm not stopping you.

JOHN doesn't move.

Feels good? If you move it feels better.

48

JOHN: What's all this about?

ASHLEY: What do you think? Revenge.

MELODY enters followed by OLIVE. OLIVE looks terrified, cowering behind, her eyes on ASHLEY as if she were a snake. MELODY looks stronger and more upright than we've seen her.

JOHN: (*Leaping up.*) I'm sorry.

MELODY: (*Ignores JOHN. To ASHLEY.*) You're going to be walking out that door in a minute hen, but see before you go, you're going tell me who you are, who sent you and what you want.

ASHLEY: You know who I am.

MELODY: I know who you're pretending to be.

OLIVE: Is it her?

MELODY: No.

JOHN: Who?

OLIVE: Is it?

MELODY: No. Olive…

ASHLEY: I'm Ashley Brown Melody. Remember me?

MELODY: OH GET OUT! OUT!

OLIVE: Is it her?

MELODY: No Olive it's not her! It's not. How can it be?

JOHN: It is but. That's Ashley…

OLIVE: (*Panicking.*) It is! It is!

MELODY: NO! Ashley's dead. Ashley died. Ashley Brown is dead.

Pause.

ASHLEY: And yet here I am. Haunting you.

OLIVE lets out a wee groan of fear and has to sit down.

JOHN: Melody......

MELODY: (*Snap.*) Baby I'll tell you all about it, just let me...

JOHN: Naw it's no that. Just to say...that...even when I'm famous, I'll never say that you're a slapper.

MELODY: Eh?

OLIVE: (*Crying into a hankie.*) Oh get him out of here. He's ruining it. Just like he ruined that barbecue. It's none of his business.

JOHN: Ruining it! How am I ruining it? And anyway, how's it any of *her* business?

MELODY: It just is.

JOHN: How?

OLIVE: (*To JOHN.*) Keep out of it you!

JOHN: Or what?

OLIVE: Or I'll give another tea in the face!

JOHN: Just you try it!

OLIVE: I will!

MELODY: Be quiet! The pair of you. If anyone's getting scalded it's madam here. So you'd better tell us the score hen or it's goodbye public school smile, hello skin grafts.

ASHLEY: You don't scare me at all.

MELODY: Oh don't I? John baby, boil the kettle please.

JOHN: What really?

MELODY: Yes please.

JOHN: See if you are scalding someone. You put sugar in the kettle. It stops the skin growing back. I saw it on *ER*.

OLIVE: Oh he's relentless. Stop talking you idiot.

JOHN: Melody did you hear…

MELODY: She's upset John.

JOHN: Aye but why? What's going on? Tell me.

ASHLEY: (*The envelope.*) This is what's going on.

MELODY: And what's that?

ASHLEY: This is the proof Melody. This is the proof that it was all your fault.

OLIVE: *What* is it?

JOHN: It's the proof that…what is it?

MELODY: It's nothing. It's a hoax or it's blackmail or it's…it's nothing. I'll call the police.

ASHLEY: After what you did? I doubt it.

MELODY: I've done nothing.

ASHLEY: Well let's see shall we? We're running a bit late but it shouldn't matter. This envelope is sealed with wax and blood…

JOHN: Eeew gadz.

ASHLEY: That's standard practice. (*Hands over the envelope.*) You've to break the seal and read the contents aloud.

MELODY: And what are the contents if you don't mind me asking?

ASHLEY: (*Shrugs.*) You'll see.

MELODY: You don't even know.

ASHLEY: You will read the contents aloud. You will face your guilt and I will walk away from my cage forever.

JOHN: I thought your cage was open now?

ASHLEY: It's open but I've yet to walk away.

MELODY: Listen you, I don't need to face my guilt or… my guilt is (*Gestures as if to say 'all around me' but then shakes that off.*) … I've… I've done nothing. Everybody knows what happened and everybody knows it wasn't my fault.

ASHLEY: Everybody?

Pause.

MELODY: (*Deep breath.*) John, in 1987 I was arrested for kidnapping a baby.

JOHN: Oh right.

MELODY: It wasn't me that took her. I just brought her back.

ASHLEY: I was that bonnie baby.

JOHN: Did you go to jail or something?

MELODY: No. I wasn't charged.

JOHN: Was it Francis that done it?

MELODY: It was. We only had her for three days and we did her no harm. I took her back. Turned myself in, but unfortunately, I had an alibi. I couldn't have taken her, I was in hospital that day so they had to let me go. When they questioned Francis it turned out he had an alibi too. (*Indicates OLIVE.*) A week after I brought her back she died. It was on the news. Cot death. It was unrelated. No matter what anyone said. It was no-one's fault.

ASHLEY: Or so we thought.

JOHN: Right. Was that why Francis went?

MELODY: It was one of the reasons. So whoever this
person is, smirking and lying and ripping me up, she is
not Ashley Brown. Because poor wee Ashley died.

OLIVE: Can I have my last cigarette Melody?

MELODY: No hen. You need to be sharp now.

OLIVE: I believe in ghosts.

MELODY: She's not a ghost.

JOHN: Are you still going to be needing this kettle for
scalding or will I do tea?

MELODY: Leave it just now John.

ASHLEY: Open it up Melody, time's running on.

OLIVE: I'm surrounded by ghosts each and every day.

JOHN: It's the jazz fags. Last week she was surrounded by
rainbows.

OLIVE: I know all about ghosts. The first one, a dead king,
grabbed me at the Garden Party. He said: 'Everybody
has a price to pay'. I threw down my plate, screamed in
Prince Andrew's face and fled. But I've never forgotten.
And here she is, to collect that debt! Here she is!

MELODY: (*To ASHLEY.*) See what you've done ya silly
wee lassie. I've changed my mind. I don't care who you
are or who sent you, I don't care what's in this, I just
want you out of here. Go on get out! Out!

ASHLEY: No! You've got to read it! Open the envelope!

MELODY: Some other time.

*MELODY grabs ASHLEY and drags her to the door. The
force of the storm blows them back a wee bit. But MELODY
is determined.*

JOHN: Wait! Wait. (*They do.*) Em…you join us live at the scene of an extraordinary…scene.

OLIVE: What's he doing now?

JOHN: Tonight, I, John…Eamonn…Rock… Hud…Rock Johnston! Tonight I, Rock Johnston will be interviewing a real live ghost on……on… *Ghost Reunions*! Stay tuned for a penetrating series of interviews and revelations.

OLIVE: What's he doing?

MELODY: I don't know. John doll, what are you doing?

JOHN: Titles. Ba da da da, bada da DA! (*American voice.*) Previously on *Ghost Reunions*… 'In 1987…'

MELODY: John! Jesus Christ. Stop that and help me get her out of here.

JOHN: Just…we'll do this quickly and then…

MELODY: No. Now. Please.

ASHLEY: Can't you see, he doesn't want me to go Melody. I wonder why? You can't keep him here forever it's not fair. He's young. It's only natural. Hence the tap dance.

JOHN: (*Normal, to ASHLEY, oblivious.*) That was like my introduction and everything, and it was live so…but I can do studio too. Do you want to see an interview? I'm very versatile.

ASHLEY: I'll bet you are darling.

OLIVE: She had her hand down his shirt.

ASHLEY: I had more than that.

MELODY: I'm not worried, just get out!

ASHLEY: He had a hard on Melody. You worried now?

MELODY: (*Smaller.*) Get out. Leave us alone. Don't let a little weather stop you.

JOHN: Weather!

ASHLEY: I've told you. I'm going nowhere. You will break the seal and read the contents aloud…

JOHN: There's a cold front rising up from the west, that's going to turn cold and wet pretty quickly…

ASHLEY: You will face your guilt and I will walk away from my cage. *Then* I can go. He was very specific about that.

JOHN: For those of you in the south expect a hurricane of biblical proportions which will destroy everything in its wake.

MELODY: Wait. You said 'He'.

JOHN: That was normal and extreme. I can do both. Versatile.

MELODY: 'He said.' Are they out there now? Is that it? Who's out there?

OLIVE: Oh it's her boyfriend Melody. I remember it. I was pretending not to listen but I was.

JOHN: As usual.

MELODY has a look outside.

OLIVE: Don't go out there he's a postman!

MELODY: There's no-one. (*The power has switched.*) You've been abandoned.

ASHLEY: Yeah right.

MELODY: See for yourself.

ASHLEY: Yeah I totally get it. He hasn't abandoned me. It's all part of the…em…part of the plan.

MELODY: Where is he then? Where is he?

ASHLEY: Well, duh! I *have* to do this alone! Phil says the only way I can be an adult is to have a conclusion to my childhood. And once I'm an adult he'll see me as an equal and commit, so obviously he can't *be* here can he? These are *my* unresolveds. And he's not abandoned me because once I'm in and you've read out whatever it is I simply phone him and he tells me what to do or whatever. It's just like, common sense.

MELODY: Get him. I want the organ grinder not the monkey.

ASHLEY: I'm grinding the organ.

OLIVE: It's the boyfriend Melody. He came up with whole idea. He's an old man. He opened her cage.

MELODY: So where is this weirdo postman?

ASHLEY: He's an artist. You wouldn't understand him Melody. Stick to your little boys. He's a genius actually.

MELODY: Oh I see. I get it now. The teenage crush on the older guy.

ASHLEY: It's not a crush it's love.

MELODY: I'll bet it is.

ASHLEY: You don't know anything about it. You've never loved like we have. No-one has.

MELODY: 'Never loved.' Oh my God. Only a teenager would say something like that.

ASHLEY: Well you haven't.

MELODY: See the love that you've got for whatsisname…

JOHN: Phil.

MELODY: That big teenage love. It disappears. Something'll happen. It always does. And oh my God your heart'll break and you'll want to die but guess what? (*Hard.*) You get over it. But you already know he doesn't love you the way you love him, don't you? You can tell by the way he moves away from you in bed that he doesn't love you. By the things he asks you to do.

ASHLEY: He does love me…

MELODY: He's using you, and you know it, twisting your arm…

ASHLEY: Shut the fuck up…

MELODY: And you know it.

ASHLEY: Shut up!

MELODY: He's forcing you, putting you in danger, just to abandon you. He's bad.

ASHLEY: Bad? You can talk. What you did to my family. Taking a baby away from us for three days and then returning her just to let her die, that's not bad? You killed her. You killed me.

MELODY: We didn't kill you, you just died. I'm a good person. It was sad that's all.

ASHLEY: No, that's not all. Sad was just the start of it. It was much more than sadness. And my family has to live with all those things that are much more than sadness and you just walk away. Well someone has to take the blame for that. Someone apart from me, because it wasn't my fault. It wasn't!

Pause.

OLIVE: Melody. It's the wee girl with the pram. It's the sister.

MELODY: Aye. It is.

57

ASHLEY: I'm not. I'm Ashley. I'm… I'm Ashley.

MELODY: Okay then. Ashley. You had a sister didn't you? Maybe three or four years older than you. She was looking after the pram in the hospital when Francis took you wasn't she? What was her name again?

ASHLEY: Annie.

MELODY: And what does Annie do now?

ASHLEY: Annie does nothing.

MELODY: She must do something.

ASHLEY: She's not allowed out. Never has been.

MELODY: She must go to school? College?

ASHLEY: No. Annie wasn't allowed to go school. Too risky. College? Yeah right.

MELODY: What about friends?

ASHLEY: Friends! What Annie? Not Annie. No friends, no birthday parties, no majorettes, no nothing. Just her, some books and two terrified people.

MELODY: She must miss you.

ASHLEY: It's not that. How can you like, miss a baby? Anyone says they miss a baby is lying. They miss the life the baby would've had. All the adventures it would've had and shared with them. That's what they're sad about. They're grieving for themselves. (*Big pause. Matter of fact.*) I didn't like having a wee sister so I just gave him the pram when he asked for it. So what.

Pause.

MELODY: How did you find me?

ASHLEY: You've got a website.

JOHN: Melody?

MELODY: John, whatever it is, just…just…

JOHN: I was just going to say that I'm on your side. That's all. I am. And if folk wanted a cup of tea or that, I'll do it.

JOHN does the teas.

MELODY: Thank you. Thanks John.

OLIVE: Boil it.

JOHN: Em…

MELODY: She can have one if she wants one.

ASHLEY: I'll phone him and then…em…the rain is… phone's off.

JOHN: Sugar? Cookery show…add a touch of sugar if you prefer a sweeter drink. Or for the more adventurous… salt.

MELODY: John.

JOHN: Okay okay.

OLIVE: (*To ASHLEY.*) I remember Francis crying when he talked about you.

MELODY: Olive.

OLIVE: Well he did. Guilt was cancer to him. It always is to pure people.

MELODY: (*To ASHLEY.*) We didn't hurt her. We just looked at her. Cuddled her. But it wasn't right. She didn't cuddle back. I think she knew we were wrong. So I…

JOHN: Tea.

JOHN hands out the teas.

MELODY: I've said sorry before. But if you want, I can say it again. It wasn't easy you know. I didn't just walk away. But it's done and on we go. You've got to see the good in what you've got right now and put on a cheery face or else why bother? I look at everything I've got and say 'everything will be alright', and I believe it. I do. But you've got to work at it. You've got to *make* that happy ending. And you'll never get there if you're tangled up in the bad things you did and the mistakes you made all those years ago. I'm burning off my tattoos and I'm starting again. That's the only way hen. So I'll say it to your face and mean it: I'm sorry. But deep down I believe that the night-times of the past are best forgotten by day.

ASHLEY's mug drops to the floor and shatters.

ASHLEY: The night-times of the past are best forgotten by day.

MELODY: What? It's just something I say.

ASHLEY unbuttons her top. She stands in her bra. Just above her heart there is a bandage. She takes off the bandage. It hurts her, the wound is fresh. MELODY comes close to see. It's a new tattoo.

MELODY: (*Reading the tattoo.*) 'The night…'

ASHLEY: I had it done two days ago.

MELODY takes off her top. Tattoos completely cover her arms like green sleeves. The bottom half of these on her right arm have been blasted off but the red outlines are still visible. The tattoos read things like 'Gene Vincent' and lots of Rockabilly slogans which were about during the brief 80s revival. The word 'Francis' can also be clearly read. There is only one tattoo on her torso. It's on her heart.

ASHLEY: (*Touching and reading MELODY's tattoo.*) 'The night-times of the past are…' Phil wanted me to…it's from one of his poems.

MELODY: The poem's called 'Kiss, Cuddle and Torture'.

ASHLEY: Yes.

Pause. Then…

OLIVE: (*Leaping up.*) It's Francis. It's Francis! Francis is back!

Half a beat for a big breath and then in panic, and with no forethought, OLIVE throws her tea in JOHN's face. Down he goes…

JOHN: Aaaaargh!!!!

Blackout as JOHN hits the carpet.

3

Again, some time has passed. The three women are sitting drinking tea, in their own worlds. JOHN has the cloth on one side of his face again and is at the window. He has the mirror from before and occasionally uses it to look out the window for Francis, like a cowboy in a shootout. MELODY holds the envelope in front of her, unopened.

OLIVE: I heard him leave but I didn't get up. I couldn't get out my bed. My heart had broken. Cracked like a paving stone tapped by a mallet. All the things in life which require effort – pleasure, passion, wit and thought – are impossible when your heart is cracked. And it's also very hard to get out of bed.

JOHN: I cannae see anything. Mind you I've only got one good eye cos of the *scalding*! My face was my livelihood. That's gone. No apology.

MELODY: You're fine. Sit down.

OLIVE: But even as I listened to him sneak out at four in the morning, making all those noises people make when they're trying to be quiet, I was happy…

JOHN: Wait a minute, wait a minute…

OLIVE: Because I'm unable to love someone whilst they are in the same room as me. When people are with me I get annoyed, I get tired, I tell them to leave me alone. Then they go, and I can't live with the pain. I love in retrospect. I love what I've imagined they were. Illusions. Then it's too late. And now I am but the final part of the Sphinx's riddle.

JOHN: Nah. That's just a…wee dog.

OLIVE: So I said goodbye under my breath and never got over it. I think we all have one great goodbye in our lives. One farewell that's so harsh, so sore, that we never really get over it. And every goodbye we say after that, no-matter how trivial, in some way reminds us of that great one. We may only feel one millionth of the pain, but it's pain none the less.

ASHLEY: Fuck it! (*To the phone.*) Where are you? You… you…there's no word to describe him.

JOHN: Dobber.

ASHLEY: I'm going to kill him. I'm going to… (*Mimes a brutal strangulation or castration or something.*) …fucking… fuck…fucking…die…DIE!

OLIVE: Did he mention me?

JOHN: Did he mention me?

ASHLEY: I… I can't remember. I can't…believe it.

JOHN: It was only an hour ago, how can you not remember? Did he mention me in a fight and/or a murder situation?

MELODY: There's not going to be a fight.

ASHLEY: He mentioned Melody. And he said there might be an old woman. That's all.

OLIVE: That's all?

JOHN: Didnae mention me though?

ASHLEY: Only on the phone. When Melody wasn't here he said to go after you.

JOHN: Shit. 'After me.' That means fighting. He means fighting!

ASHLEY: No. Just…get you away from Melody. Just fuck things up for you, you know.

JOHN: How?

ASHLEY: First I was just to seduce you but then…then I came up with the idea of pretending to have connections in TV.

JOHN: Pretending?

ASHLEY: To, like, make you leave or something. I dunno.

JOHN: Oh.

ASHLEY: I'm sorry. He…

JOHN: It's alright.

JOHN looks devastated. MELODY goes to him.

MELODY: Are you okay baby?

JOHN: Aye. I… I was just kidding on anyway.

MELODY: Well. You deserve something else. You should be a presenter. You will be.

JOHN: I won't though. It's all kid on isn't it?

MELODY: Ach John. You're just a wee boy aren't you?

JOHN: I'm a grown man.

MELODY: Aye okay.

JOHN: Melody…see if there is a fight who would you want to win?

MELODY: There isnae going to be a fight. It's Francis! He just wants to stir things up. (*To ASHLEY.*) Right?

JOHN: You said he was violent.

MELODY: Not that violent. Not that type of violent.

JOHN: Do you want to see him?

MELODY: I dunno baby.

JOHN: I will fight him. I'll be a man after that.

OLIVE: It'd take more than that to make you a man.

JOHN: What did you say?

OLIVE: Oh nothing.

JOHN: Why are you still here by the way? Golden boy's back have you not heard? You've been looking out that window as if he was going to walk out the sea and ring that bell for years. Well, your big day's arrived, and yet for some reason you're still sitting there moaning. Looking like you're about to do a bungee jump. So what's the matter eh? Why no tearful reunion and slow motion running? Eh? Why are *you* shiteing it he's back?

MELODY: John leave her alone it's a shock for her.

JOHN: Naw! I've had to listen to her spouting crap about how ace Francis is since the day I moved in here. 'Francis's first word was monograph', 'Francis can dislocate his shoulders at will', 'Francis was Melody's true love and he's coming back to steal her away'. But it was all crap. I don't think she even likes Francis.

OLIVE: You haven't a clue how I feel about Francis. You don't have the capability to comprehend how I feel about Francis. Because you don't feel anything beyond tantrums and sulks. Francis and I… Francis and I are more complex than anything you'll ever understand.

ASHLEY: It's ringing!

ASHLEY throws the phone down as if bitten.

JOHN: (*To OLIVE.*) Well, if you and him are so close, why don't you give him a bell and see what his fucking game is?

MELODY: Maybe someone should talk to him.

ASHLEY: Why?

MELODY: To let him know his plan hasn't worked.

OLIVE: Hasn't it?

ASHLEY: Well I'm not speaking to him. I never want to see him again. Unless he's covered in boiling water with sugar on top. Yeah I'd like to pour that kettle all over him. Scald the liar. Burn away all those lies. And then I'd like to open up *his* 'cage', and pour the rest of it over his fucking…dobber.

MELODY: It should be me. I should do it.

MELODY gets the phone. ASHLEY gets the number ready for her.

What'll I say?

OLIVE: Tell him he's been banished from Thebes. He'll know what it means.

JOHN: Tell him to fuck off. He'll know what that means 'n aw.

ASHLEY: Tell him that if his plan was to crush a woman, to brand his name on her soul forever, to have her tattooed on the heart, then it's a victory. Tell him to celebrate. But tell him, if this is something to do with burning things away so he can be free, then he's failed. Cos I still love him. Tell him that.

MELODY: Great.

MELODY dials. She hangs up. Can't do it.

JOHN: Here give us it. I'll just tell him to get tae. I'm the man. He doesnae have a single fucking…it's ringing…… (*Long beat. Hangs up suddenly.*) What'll I say?

ASHLEY: Did he answer?

JOHN: Aye.

MELODY: No. We're not phoning him. We're not even seeing him. That's what he wants. (*To ASHLEY.*) You'll…you'll have to go.

ASHLEY: What?

MELODY: I'm really sorry and everything. I know it's been a nightmare and that you blame me but I can't do this. You have to go.

ASHLEY: I don't blame you anymore though. I blame him. Where will I go?

MELODY: Go to Francis. You love him.

ASHLEY: I love Phil. And he doesn't exist, so I can never see him again. Don't you understand that? It's impossible. Phil's a dream and Francis is real. But Francis wants to burn me away. Why would I go to him?

MELODY: You'd get over it.

ASHLEY: Have you?

MELODY: Go home then. To your mother.

ASHLEY: I don't want to live there anymore. I'm like a prisoner. I don't even have a TV.

MELODY: They're just worried. It's natural.

ASHLEY: No. They blame me. They think it was my fault because I was in charge of the pram.

MELODY: Ach don't be daft, you were tiny, you shouldn't have been left with a pram.

ASHLEY: It was my fault she was taken. It was my fault she died.

MELODY: But it wasn't pet. You know that. Some babies just die. Olive. Do you remember what you told me in the hospital? You said that some babies are born with the wrong size of soul. Remember? Too big. They can't live with the sadness like we can so they close their eyes and go home. But even though they don't stay long they make our souls bigger. Everyone who caught their eye.

OLIVE: I never said that.

MELODY: You did. Francis was there. Just before…you did.

OLIVE: I didn't say that.

ASHLEY: There's no soul at home at all. They hate me there. I don't want hate anymore. I just want this. Sitting in every night in your slippers drinking tea. I want *real* things. Please. I could stay here. For a few days anyway…

OLIVE: She can't stay!

JOHN: How can she no?

OLIVE: Well…well…there's no room.

JOHN: There's your room. You'll be away with Francis.

MELODY: John.

OLIVE: I won't.

JOHN: Aye but *why* won't you? I thought that was the plan?

OLIVE: He only wants her to stay so he can have his perverted way with her. Him and his filth and his (*The PC.*) *pictures*! And now he'll have her here right under your nose, oh Melody could you be as naïve as that?

MELODY: Calm down Olive no-one's saying…

OLIVE: And how can you believe a thing she says? She came into this house to cause us harm. She had her hands all over him.

ASHLEY: That wasn't me...

OLIVE: Lying about who she was, lying about everything. She was evil ten minutes ago how can she be nice now? I'll bet...eh... I'll bet they're...aye... I'll bet they're in on it together. Talking all night on the computer, planning this together. Check! Go on Melody! I'll bet they are. Get your...where's that bit of paper... (*Looks down the side of the chair.*)

MELODY: What is it hen? Why are you...?

OLIVE: The bit of paper! The paper from the paper! For the love of God the thing, the *thing*, from the, from the paper. I read it, about DOS and CD. THE PAPER!

MELODY: Oh aye, it's here, calm...

OLIVE: Yes. Take it and see what they've been planning. They have and you'll see. She can't stay if they've been planning it under your nose. The things they'll do...

JOHN: We won't! I won't. I never...

MELODY: Olive...

OLIVE: Look at him. They'll end up together. They will! You know already don't you? He'll leave you for her if she stays. It happened to me I know. He...they'll... they'll just go. Stolen from you. She can't stay... there's...there's – don't make me go. I don't want to go. I can't. It's too late. It's too late. I want to stay. Please. I want to stay here please. Don't make me go.

MELODY goes to her and tries to give her a cuddle. OLIVE pulls away.

MELODY: Oh Olive of course you can stay. No-one said you had to go.

OLIVE: It's too late for me to go anywhere else.

MELODY: Ach hen. Of course you can stay. You're family.

OLIVE: I'm not.

MELODY: I know, but you feel like that to me.

OLIVE: You don't feel like that to me. I *don't* like it here. Don't think I want to stay for love. I staying because I can't go. I don't have another move in me.

MELODY: But… I'm sure you like it here sometimes eh? You must.

OLIVE: No.

MELODY: You do.

OLIVE: I don't. I don't even like you.

MELODY: Olive… I'm standing right here. I do have… *feelings.*

OLIVE: You never knew me before Francis. If you knew who I was then, you'd pity me now. I had languages. I had lovers. I had this place stunned. They'd never seen anyone quite like me and they never will again. But now I have nothing. I'm just a wee old woman like all the others. It counts for nothing, absolutely *nothing* in the end. It's amazing how little say you have in where you die. By the time it becomes a factor you've long since washed up on a foreign shore, miles from home, all your spirit drained.

MELODY: I didn't realise this was such a misery for you.

OLIVE: Well.

MELODY: Only, I seem to remember you turning up at me and Francis' flat in Glasgow begging us to come back here. And we did. For you. Split the band up. We even moved you in with us after all the tears. And I thought I was being really kind to you. Looking after you even when he'd long gone.

OLIVE: Looking after me? You control me. Rationing my cigarettes to keep me in line. Punishing me…

MELODY: They're dangerous. And illegal! I could go to jail for buying that stuff for you!

OLIVE: Punishing me. Both of us. To keep us here.

MELODY: Punishing…?

OLIVE: And I stay. Mouth shut. As penance. As payback. As God knows what.

MELODY: You've never said…you've never mentioned…

OLIVE: You've never asked. You talk *at* me. Like I'm a child.

MELODY: Well there's plenty of things I'd liked to have talked to you about but I don't. Plenty. But I don't. To spare you…

OLIVE: You don't know anything about me. You'll never know me.

MELODY: Oh I know you.

OLIVE: Melody. You are a fucking victim. You hear me? A fucking victim. And I'll always pity you for that. Because you don't even realise. So you'll never know me.

Pause.

MELODY: If you hate it here so much you can just go. GO! All of you! You're all only here cos you hate somewhere else.

JOHN: I want to be here.

ASHLEY: So do I.

MELODY: Ah…who cares…why am I… I'm just what people have until something better comes along. And I can't keep this up. It's…so…exhausting.

JOHN: Melody I do want to be here. With you. Honest. Keep a cheery face. 'Everything'll be alright.' Tea? Right?

ASHLEY: Yeah, tea. Everything will be alright.

MELODY: Right.

JOHN puts the kettle on.

OLIVE: Don't listen to them. They're stolen property. Forgeries. In love with their kidnapper. You stole us. Just like you stole that baby…

MELODY: It was Francis that stole her, I brought her back.

OLIVE: But it was your idea wasn't it?

MELODY: No.

OLIVE: Oh it was. I remember. I remember the letter. You gave him a letter. A suicide note that said you'd kill yourself unless you left the hospital with a child. Like a real mother. Francis showed it to me and I'll wager my life that if I open that envelope I'll see it again. He didn't want to do it, but he felt guilty and he was scared of you running out on him. He was scared that something would happen to that wee baby too and he was right. Something did happen. He was so shattered, so full of revulsion at what you'd made him do he ran. Ran from you!

MELODY: Stupid old woman. Stupid, stupid, stupid old woman. I can't believe you're sticking with all that rubbish, even now, with him somewhere out there and you in here. My God, I've let you gibber on about this imaginary Francis who glows in the dark and loves you and is coming to save you for years, but I'm not having it now. Because you know fine well it's all crap. It's a bloody fantasy. He wasn't running from me he was running from you. And you know it. That's why you're sitting there terrified. You know he hates you for what you did to him.

OLIVE: I did nothing to him.

MELODY: You wouldn't leave him alone. You were obsessed with him. (*To JOHN and ASHLEY.*) When he was ill he would get into her bed. He'd sleep beside her.

OLIVE: I never forced him. He wanted to.

MELODY: A grown man spending the night in bed with his own mother!

JOHN: Gadz.

MELODY: You smothered him and he hated you for it. He never had a chance to be normal with you as his mother. The looks she'd give him! It was sickening. No wonder he lost the plot.

OLIVE: You were just jealous. Jealous that he'd rather sleep in my bed than yours.

JOHN: Fucking gadz man!

OLIVE: And if he *was* running from me why did he spend his last night in *my* bed.

MELODY: And why are you still sitting there instead of in Francis' arms? Because you know what kind of a man he is. And you know that it's all your fault.

OLIVE: It's something you'll never understand.

MELODY: What?

OLIVE: A mother's love. (*Pause.*) You were jealous then and you're jealous now.

73

Pause.

MELODY: Jealous? Every single day I think about where I'd be if there'd never been a Francis. But I motor on all smiles and optimism. I make do. I take any wee bit of happiness that's going and never complain. Well I'm fucking complaining now. I wish I was like a computer and could just delete everything. All my history gone. Every day. Every thing I do. It's written on me. All over me. (*Shows her tattoos.*) And just when things had settled, Francis returns! With ghosts in tow. Mother's love! Aye right. Look at you, you wish he'd just disappear. I'm with her. I'd like to scald him. Burn him out of existence. Burn it all out of existence. Everything. In fact that's not a bad idea.

JOHN: What you doing?

MELODY: Looking for sugar.

JOHN: How?

MELODY: Stops the skin growing back. I think all traces should be removed.

JOHN: Melody doll? Are you alright?

MELODY: I will be. Just let me burn off these tattoos and we can have a nice wee cup of tea.

JOHN: You're kidding.

MELODY: Nope. I want all traces gone.

JOHN: Don't be daft. It'd be agony.

MELODY: I'm used to it.

ASHLEY: Melody for fuck sake don't listen to her. You're not a victim. You're strong.

MELODY: You don't know me.

ASHLEY: You're stronger than this.

MELODY: I'm not.

ASHLEY: Think of everything you've got.

MELODY: I've got delusions. And I've got tattoos. In a minute I'll just have delusions.

MELODY lifts the kettle.

JOHN: Don't Melody please!

JOHN tries to grab the kettle. They struggle a bit.

What do you want doll? Whatever it is I'll do it. Just put it down.

The kettle drops. Water splashes him. He shrieks and drops to the floor. In agony.

Aaaaaaah! The cloth!

ASHLEY gets the cloth. MELODY can see he's not really hurt. She looks at ASHLEY cradling him on the floor. She picks up the kettle and calmly mops up the mess.

MELODY: I want what she wants. I want things to be real. You know what I mean? Real. Not pretend. I want a real… I want us to be real. A real couple.

JOHN: We are a real couple.

MELODY: Then we need to have sex John.

JOHN: Now?

MELODY: Not now but soon. We need to actually have sex like normal folk. Not just cuddling. I need to feel what…she felt. Oh God sake John there's nothing…let me see…there's nothing wrong you're fine. And I know you have the urges other times too cos you're on the internet half the night looking at God knows what.

JOHN: Eh?

MELODY: Porn. You must be interested in sex looking at those pictures all night.

JOHN: But I'm not.

MELODY: Don't lie to me.

JOHN: I'm not. I swear.

MELODY: Then what? What? What are you doing that takes you out of my bed?

JOHN: I'm…talking to mum. We talk on the internet. Just…you know…talk.

MELODY: John…

JOHN: I want to be with you. Now. And not cos I'm waiting on something else coming along, but because I've chosen you. I want it back just the way it was yesterday. Even Olive. I want her to stay. We should just make it that nothing's happened. Nothing *has* happened! We should just sit down and pretend Francis isn't real and maybe he'll go away.

MELODY: For God sake John, you can't just pretend your problems aren't real and ignore them.

ASHLEY: You can. Some envelopes should never be opened.

MELODY: I cannae cope with that. I cannae go on just pretending that all is well. I'm sorry but I can't. I'm done with it. That's over now. Cos now I'm going to say this, out loud, and you're going to listen. Francis is out there and he's not just going to go away.

OLIVE: Yes he is. He's already gone. And he won't be back. The damage is done. John's right. So's she. We should just pretend nothing's happened. We should wipe away everything that's happened up to now and just carry on.

MELODY: But that's mad!

OLIVE: No it's not Melody. It's not. Everyone does it. Stop anyone on the street and I'd bet they're thinking about some dream or film or holiday or anything just to take their mind off their real life, which will undoubtedly be a mess. They're happy in a delusion – in love with an illusion. Just like me. Just like us. John's right.

JOHN: Aye. Look hen. Nothing's changed. The house is just the same. Same PC, same couch, same bloody kettle. We've still got jobs to go to in the morning. We're no going anywhere. Neither's Ashley, right?

ASHLEY: Annie.

JOHN: See. Whoever. She's staying. Nothing's changed right? That's what you wanted, right?

MELODY: But what about Francis? And all the things Francis wants to do to us?

OLIVE: Francis has gone away, so we can remember him however we like. Keep a cheery face.

Big pause.

JOHN: I think that boiling water's scarred me by the way.

ASHLEY: Aw let me see. Ach there's nothing wrong with you.

OLIVE: He's a baby, crying at the tiniest scratch.

JOHN: What would you know about it? Half of the things she says are wrong with her the doctor hasnae even heard of. Maybe I should have a word with the doctor about your big thumbs eh Melody? Maybe get you a thumbectomy. Thumbnoplasty.

OLIVE: The doctor's a fool. His mind has blunted dealing with morons like you weeping over a blocked nose day in day out.

JOHN: That was three times I've been scalded in one night man. That's a record for me. Agony.

OLIVE: Agony! Once you've had a child then you can talk to me about agony.

JOHN: I'll be talking to you about miracles if that ever happens, I'm a man.

ASHLEY: Well you were in the majorettes.

OLIVE: You were in the majorettes?

JOHN: Not for long. Melody how about a nice wee cup of tea eh? Then we can all put our feet up and see what's on the TV. Early night I think.

During the above MELODY has been watching them as if it was a performance she can't work out. They're a million miles away now. Out of reflex, she goes to the kitchen and boils the kettle. A car's headlights sweep the window. No-one looks. Pulses rise though...

JOHN: I can't remember, do you take sugar or not Ashley? I'm daft.

OLIVE: He is, he's a daft idiot. I hope you take it tepid, because that's the vogue in this house.

JOHN: Don't listen to her, there's something wrong with her temperatures.

OLIVE: In my youth I drank seamonkey tea in a Peking brothel, so I know all about tea temperatures. What's on the TV you?

JOHN: Probably load of rubbish eh? We've missed *The Simpsons*. We'll just sit here and watch TV eh Ashley? Be nice.

ASHLEY: Yeah.

JOHN: Yeah. Just sit here right Melody?

OLIVE: Just carrying on as usual.

JOHN: Yup.

ASHLEY: I'll stay tonight and think about going tomorrow.

OLIVE: Oh aye take your time. Plenty of room.

JOHN: Yup. Plenty.

OLIVE: There's a Z-bed.

JOHN: It's no bother.

ASHLEY: Cool.

JOHN: It's actually quite comfy for a…

> *DING DONG. There's somebody at the door.*

Z-bed.

> *Huge pause. Nobody but MELODY looks at the door. She has a strange expression on her face. As if she has been expecting this. She seems apart from the fear that Francis inspires from now on. She takes out the envelope and after a moment, plops it into the kettle, unopened.*

> *DING DONG.*

> *Nothing again from anyone. The sound of the kettle boiling rises unnaturally.*

MELODY: I suppose we should make a decision here eh?

OLIVE: We've made the decision. It's tea we want.

> *DING DONG.*

MELODY: What about me?

JOHN: Melody just make the tea!

> *DING DONG. The door handle is tried. It's locked on snub.*

ASHLEY: I don't take sugar.

79

MELODY: I do.

DING DONG.

Now there's a THUMP at the door. Another…

THUMP.

MELODY lifts the lid off the kettle. Steam rockets up. She starts to shovel spoonful after spoonful of sugar into the kettle calmly.

THUMP THUMP THUMP.

OLIVE: Whoever it is will no doubt go away. What with the storm and everything.

JOHN: Aye. We should've put up sandbags.

THUMP THUMP THUMP

DING DONG.

THUMP.

ASHLEY: Keep a cheery face. Everything'll be alright.

DING DONG DING DONG DING DONG

MELODY: (*Holding the kettle and putting on her cheery face.*) Yeah. Everything'll be alright.

DING DONG. MELODY unlocks the door.

Come in!

Blackout.

the end